mini STEPS to happiness

This book belongs to:

STARTING *steps*

God's book, the Bible, is full of wise words and instructions on how we can live great lives.

In this book we will learn about 9 important steps to happiness, also known as the fruit of the spirit.

"The fruit of the spirit is love, joy, peace, patience, kindness, goodness, faithfulness, gentleness and self-control."

(Galatians 5:22-23)

Here are 4 easy ways

to help you learn and remember what you read in this book.

Look with your eyes
1

Listen with your ears
2

Remember with your mind
3

Do it with your actions
4

step one
LOVE

Whee! I swing in the breeze.
I feel like a bird flying in the sky.

My sister let me have a turn on the swing first, even though she got here before I did. She even helped me to swing up high. That's a lot of love.

"Thank you sister!"
I want to do the same for others too.

LOVE is letting others have a turn first.

step one
LOVE

Mom asked me to feed the fish. I looked at her and answered, "Okay, Mom! I'll do it right now!"

Then she gave me a great big hug. "I'm so proud of my boy who talks with respect." she said.

It's funny, but using respect makes me feel all grown up.

LOVE is showing respect.

step one
LOVE

Today I invited Julie to my house for play. She wanted the doll that I was playing with.

I thought about it and decided to share. I played with the doll-house instead, and later on, we switched.

Things worked out great that way.

LOVE is sharing.

step one
LOVE

Grandma usually comes to visit me, but today she was sick. So I went to visit her instead.

I know that she likes chicken soup, so I asked Mom to help me prepare some.

Grandma smiled real big and said "You remembered my favorite food. Now I'm sure to get better."

LOVE is thinking of others.

step two
JOY

I'm not a rock star or a music star. I'm not any star at all, but I love to sing. I am filled with joy when I sing out loud.

Singing even helps me forget about my hurt toe or about missing a friend. And instead, I am happy and cheerful.

JOY makes me want to sing.

step two
JOY

Aren't my balloons lovely?
Such wonderful colors.

Oh no! One popped.
What will I do now?

I could get sad and do some crying.
Or I could be thankful for the two
balloons I have left to play with.
On top of it, blue and red are my
very favorite colors.

JOY helps me see the good.

step two
JOY

I don't have the latest or fanciest toys, but I don't really mind because I have a good friend to play with. I also have a rope and a nearby pond to splash in.

I am content because I have lots of fun with even a few things.

JOY makes me content.

step two
JOY

Joy is feeling happy inside even when it's not a great day. I know that the sun is always shining, even when I can't see it.

So I put on my special glasses of cheerfulness and I think of the beauty around me.

JOY keeps me positive.

step three
PEACE

Today, my family and I took a walk up the hill, far from all the noise and pollution. I sat on the soft carpet of grass and looked all around.

I heard the birds singing and the leaves rustling in the breeze. I picked some of my favorite flowers. It felt so calm and quiet. I liked that.

PEACE is finding a quiet place.

step three
PEACE

We were having a great game of ball when all of a sudden, things went wrong. The boys couldn't agree on what the score was and soon they were yelling at each other. That hurt my ears.

But instead of joining the argument, I decided to be a peacemaker. I gave an idea of how we could work things out. Soon our playing was happy again.

PEACE *finds a way to make everyone happy.*

step three
PEACE

I'm learning to write my name. I'm learning to get dressed all on my own. My brain is doing a lot of work every day.

But sometimes we need time to rest. My parents call it "taking a vacation". I get time to relax, listen to the waves and enjoy my favorite drink. It feels so peaceful.

PEACE is giving my body a rest.

step three
PEACE

Everyday I need some rest.
When I sleep my body grows and
heals. So I get all cozy under
my fluffy blanket.

Mom gives me a cuddle and kisses me
good night. Dad reads me stories and
makes me laugh. Even my kitty cat
needs a cuddle and peaceful rest.

PEACE brings me rest and comfort.

step four
PATIENCE

I love to play sports: ball games, bat games, almost any game.

First I watched my dad, then I practiced in the garden. Next I played with my friends. Finally I joined a sports team. It took a lot of patience to practice over and over. But I've gotten much better at it now.

Can you cheer for me to win?

Learning new things takes PATIENCE.

step four
PATIENCE

Sometimes I wish I could do what grown-ups do. I want to walk to places on my own, to try all the things I see. But I still have a lot to learn, so I hold Mom's hand and follow her.

I may not be able to carry a heavy bag yet, but I can carry my teddy. I may not be able to read all the signs yet, but I can understand what Mom tells me. I'm being smart by being patient and learning a little more all the time.

Waiting to grow up takes PATIENCE.

step four
PATIENCE

"Dad, can we build a toy boat together?" I asked him. Dad agreed. So we made the plans, measured, cut, screwed and glued. It was hard work and it took a long time to get it done. But look at it now!

Don't you think this boat looks great? Now we can finally enjoy it and try it out on the lake.

It takes PATIENCE to finish a job.

step four
PATIENCE

It's hard to wait for a slice of pizza. It's hard to wait for my turn with a toy. So to make it easier, I think of something that keeps me busy.

I might think of the yummy pizza my tummy will enjoy, or of all the ways I can play with my fun toy. I don't have to be worried or sad to wait. Waiting patiently can be part of the fun because I have something to look forward to.

PATIENCE is waiting cheerfully.

step five
KINDNESS

I have lots of fun flying my kite on this windy day. But then I see a boy with nothing to play with.

"Here, you can have a turn with my kite!" I tell him. We play together and it's even more fun. We take turns to hold the string and zoom the kite across the sky. It feels good to think of others. And I've even made a new friend.

KINDNESS is being friendly.

step five
KINDNESS

My school teacher helps us to read and write, and I can tell that I'm doing better already.

I wanted to do something special for her, so I asked Mom to help me bake some cookies.

Now that they're done, I'll wrap them nicely and add a thank you card. Do you think she'll like this gift?

KINDNESS is doing loving deeds.

step five
KINDNESS

I'd like to watch my favorite princess video now, but my little brother wants to look at funny animals.

"We can watch the animals first." I tell him. We see a monkey dancing and a cat doing flips. Letting others go first is part of kindness. I loved seeing my brother so happy and I enjoyed the funny animal videos too.

KINDNESS is making others happy.

step five
KINDNESS

Mom and Dad have lots of work to do. Since I already had play time, I think they could use my help with some tidying up around the house. What do you think?

I pick up the toys and I sweep the floor. I even have time to serve them milk and cookies for snack.

KINDNESS is giving a helping hand.

step six
GOODNESS

"Mom, are these finger foods?" I ask. Then I take a small bite of broccoli. It's not my favorite food, but I eat it anyway, because it's good for my body. I just pretend that it's a crunchy granola bar.

I sit nicely and say "please" and "thank you," because mealtime is pleasant when we have good manners!

GOODNESS is using good manners.

step six
GOODNESS

The sign at the zoo says: "Do not feed the animals!" I wonder why?

But it's best for me to follow the rules, even if I don't understand why.

Mom says that following rules helps to keep us safe. That sounds like a good idea. I wear a seat belt to be safe in the car. I wash my hands to help keep sickness away. I see that rules are for my good.

GOODNESS is
following the rules.

step six
GOODNESS

I was having fun playing with my cars and building roads with my blocks. But then Mom called me for dinner.

"Oh, no! I don't want to stop now." But I decided to obey, stay cheerful and put my toys away.

Mom worked hard to prepare the food, and it sure made my tummy feel good.

GOODNESS is obeying right away.

step six
GOODNESS

My friends are playing barefoot outside.
But Mom told me to keep my shoes on,
because I may step on something sharp.

Should I do what my friends are doing, or
should I listen to Mom?

Mom knows what's good for me.
And she used to be a little girl too.
So I choose to keep my slippers on
and my feet stay safe and clean.

GOODNESS is making wise choices.

step seven
FAITHFULNESS

Mom has never forgotten to serve yummy meals each day. That's being faithful.

It's my big "grown-up" job to feed the cat every day. He would not be happy if I forgot.

I am faithful to do my part and to take care of our family and home too.

FAITHFULNESS is doing my job each day.

step seven
FAITHFULNESS

My friend invited me over for play.
I really want to go, but first I have some homework to finish. I find a quiet spot and practice my reading.

I read loud enough so that my dog can hear. "Woof! Woof!" he says.

I think that means I'm doing good. And when I'm all done, I get to go and play. Fun fun, here I come!

I am FAITHFUL to finish work before play.

step seven
FAITHFULNESS

I took out my roads and dumped all the cars on the floor. I find my very favorite ones that way. Vroom, vroom, vroom! That means they go really fast.

When the clock rings, that means it's time to get ready for bed. I drive the cars into the toy box at high speed. Vroom, vroom! I make sure no cars are left out. That way I can find them for next play time. That's being faithful.

I am FAITHFUL to put things away.

step seven
FAITHFULNESS

I want to be a ballerina, so I put on my special dress for dance lessons. Sometimes I don't feel like going to dance school, but if I want to be a ballerina, I need to practice often.

So I dance every day, sometimes with friends at dance class and sometimes at home with my dollies. I'm getting pretty good at spinning now.

I am FAITHFUL to practice often.

step eight
GENTLENESS

I love to explore outdoors with Mom and Dad. We walk in the forest, we wade through puddles. We climb rocks or we roll down grassy hills. Sometimes I even get to ride on Dad's shoulders.

To find lots of little animals, we need to stay very still and quiet. Otherwise they get scared away. Look! I think this butterfly really likes me. Hmm, I wonder who else I scare away when I'm too loud.

GENTLENESS is staying calm and quiet.

step eight
GENTLENESS

Our family is preparing for a new baby. I hope I'll make a good older sister. First I get to practice on my dollies. I carry them gently. I talk with a quiet, sweet voice. I sing them to sleep. I give them a bottle when they get hungry.

I need to be gentle.
Baby will love being with me that way.

step eight
GENTLENESS

"Lunch time!" Mom gently calls.
Oh no, my playing plans are ruined,
and I feel a bit upset.

Things didn't go my way, but I
don't get angry and yell. That
wouldn't work out very well.
Instead, I use gentle words.
"Okay Mom. I'll be right there!"

GENTLENESS is not getting angry.

step eight
GENTLENESS

Here's my super cool remote control car. It can go real fast. But sometimes it crashes into doors and walls. At least this toy has a strong bumper to keep it from breaking.

But my other toys don't have bumpers to protect them. So I don't crash them around or let them fall to the ground. I want them to last me a long time.

GENTLENESS is taking good care of things.

step nine
SELF-CONTROL

I have homework to finish up. I have playtime with friends. At times I even get to play some electronic games.

But there is a time for everything. So I make sure that I don't do something too long. It's not so easy to stop when I'm in the middle of having fun, but I'm learning to control myself and to be a good boss over my body.

SELF-CONTROL is keeping track of time.

step nine
SELF-CONTROL

I control myself by choosing foods that are healthy for me. Fruits are a great snack when my tummy wants something sweet. What is your favorite fruit?

I don't always like what's on my plate. Sometimes green leaves don't make me feel too great. But I eat some of them anyway because I want to give my body what is good for it.

SELF-CONTROL is choosing what is good for me.

step nine
SELF-CONTROL

When I wake up in the morning, I get myself ready even before Mom asks me to. At school, I pay attention to the teacher even when she's not looking at me. And after meals, I brush my teeth without being reminded.

Do you know why?

I feel proud building good habits and learning to do things on my own.

SELF-CONTROL is building good habits.

step nine
SELF-CONTROL

On our way home, it started to rain. Oh no! My dress is getting wet with splashes of mud, the sky is grey, the view is... Wait a minute, this isn't making me feel very good. I don't have to let the gloomy day make me feel sad.

Instead, I can be glad we brought umbrellas. I have boots to splash in the puddles. I can sing in the rain, just like the birds. And when we get home, we can have my favorite warm drink. Yay!

SELF-CONTROL is using the right words.

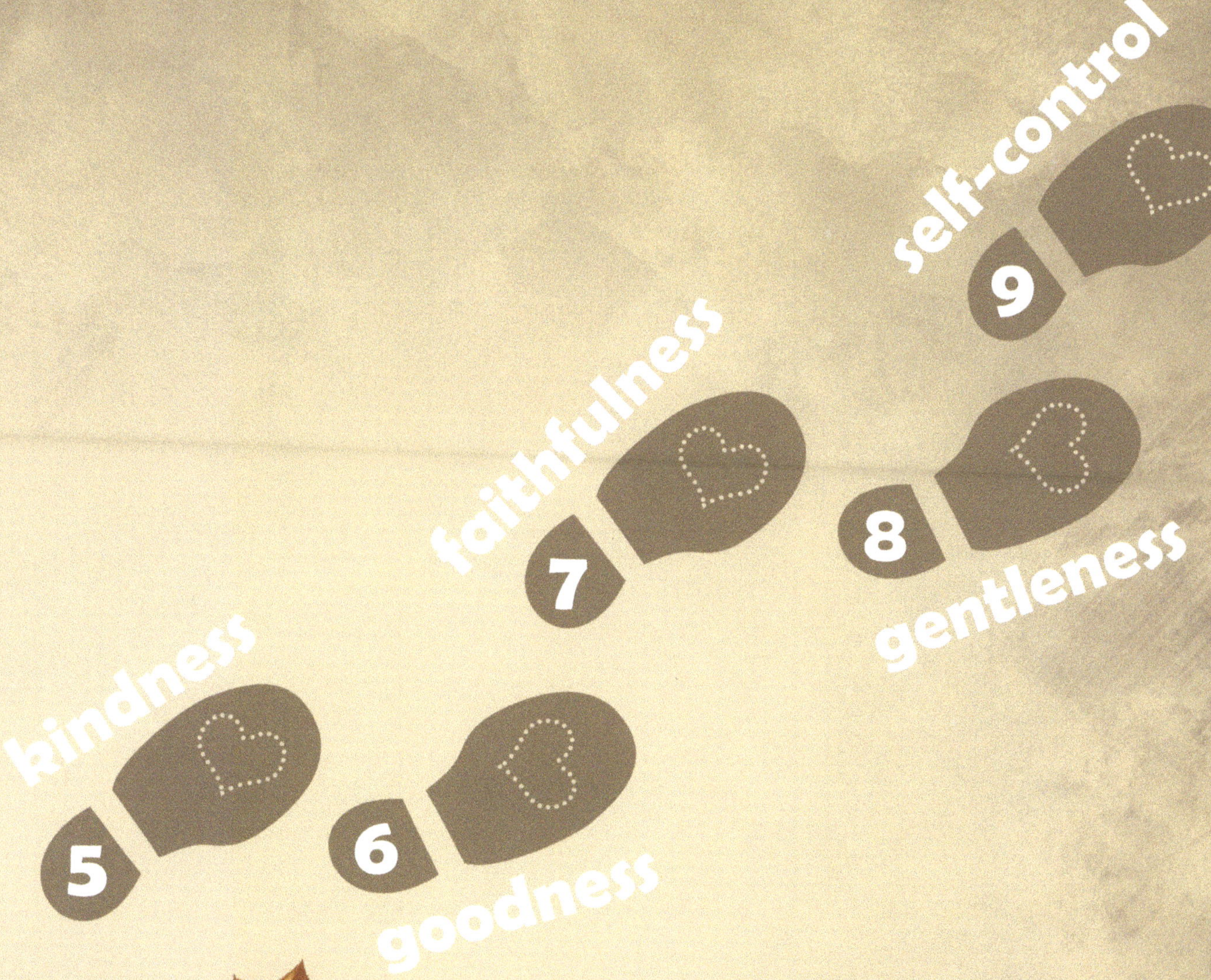

kindness 5

goodness 6

faithfulness 7

gentleness 8

self-control 9

Do you remember the

4 STEPS TO LEARNING?

Find them at the beginning of this book and review them.

Then try out one of the examples from each of these 9 steps. Place a sticker on the shoe prints once you're done.

More titles available:

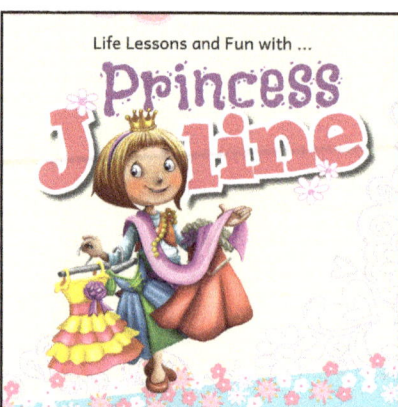

Published by iCharacter Ltd. (Ireland)
www.iCharacter.org
By Agnes and Salem de Bezenac
Illustrated by Agnes de Bezenac
Colored by Sonny
Copyright. All rights reserved.

Get FREE downloads

Copyright © 2016 iCharacter Limited. All rights reserved. No part of this book may be reproduced in any form or by any electronic or mechanical means, including information storage and retrieval systems, without written permission from the publisher or author, except in the case of a reviewer, who may quote brief passages embodied in critical articles or in a review.

www.ingramcontent.com/pod-product-compliance
Lightning Source LLC
Chambersburg PA
CBHW040002080526
44586CB00027B/2858